Leaderhood

Augusta Francis Publishing

Felix Asade

Cover illustration:
Samuella Asade (*Sammy Graphics*)

Dedication

This book is dedicated to all Leaders: past, present, and future.

Contents

Introduction

Leadership remains one of the study areas of the Social Sciences that has been largely studied from time immemorial. It is fascinating to note however that considerable interest in knowing more about leadership has been directed at studying leaders, their attributes, personalities, and styles. Thus, much of what is known and taught about leadership has been based on how some leaders in the past have behaved or on how they emerged as leaders and so on and so forth.

What has so far been taught about leadership are mostly theories of Management and gives the impression that leadership is an offshoot of Management, and the art of managing people, especially in business settings. Business Leadership theories derived from Management, form the bulk of knowledge about leadership whereas there are more areas of leadership that should be open to further studies and research like the political aspects of leadership, the social aspects of leadership, and much more.

Leaderhood seeks to show what leadership is, beyond its being treated as an offspring of Management and its heavy reliance on Management theories. Leaderhood brings leadership from a different perspective and addresses important issues like what leadership is by exploring the tangible and intangible aspects of leadership; how leadership occurs through the attainment of leaderhood; the activation, growth and development of leadership; leadership fit, leadership equilibrium and leadership failure.

Leadership is more than activities and goes beyond getting people to achieve goals.

1

THE LEADERSHIP ACTIVATION PERSPECTIVE

LEADERHOOD

Different leadership ideas have proponents, and copious literature, but there is an alternative explanation of leadership which looks to explain leadership in a different way, and that is the **Leaderhood Theory** through its **Leadership Activation Perspective**.

Leadership Activation Perspective holds that **leadership is the outward manifestation of leaderhood initiatives occurring by the intersection of *thoughts*, awareness, *concern*, and action.** Leadership is attainable by everyone that has attained leaderhood and they only need to activate the innate leadership abilities in them *by thinking, by seeking information, by analysing and by acting appropriately.*

The Leadership activation perspective neither sees leadership as a process nor special traits, but rather as a resource common to all human beings and requires a process of activation. In this view, leadership is not a process of influencing people but involves a process. Otherwise, leadership would be reduced to the process of influencing negotiations. While leading people could involve negotiations, leadership goes beyond negotiation or the use of power to influence people.

WHAT IS LEADERSHIP?

Leadership has been represented variously and while some discuss leadership in the context of its relationship with other people, others mostly associate leadership with goal setting and performance (Piccolo and Buengeler, 2013) or in its affective nature as the art of influencing others to work (Ibrahim and Daniel, 2019), or in relation to influence generally (Cheng,2002) or as the result of some traits (Bolden, 2004).

While goals setting and goals performance, are part of what leaders do, leadership is more than goals or performances. There are elements of influence in leading people, but leadership is not just about influence. And it is not about some special traits peculiar to a few people. What then is leadership?

According to Leaderhood Theory, based on the Leadership Activation Perspective, Leadership is about the attainment and application of leaderhood and can be defined as:

The transformable innate resource in every human being that makes leading effective when it is activated.

Leadership as a resource moves across four stages as follows:

DORMANT STAGE	ACTIVATED STAGE	APPLICATION STAGE	DEVELOPMENT STAGE
Latent leadership	Leaderhood	Visible leadership	Quality Leadership
		(With or without position)	(Skills Acquisition)

1. Leadership is an invisible innate instrument or resource, in every human being, existing first in its natural unrefined state. This is **latent leadership** possessed by everyone.
2. Leadership can transform or change from latent status to active status when it becomes activated, and this signifies the attainment of the leaderhood status. (Internalised leadership)
3. Attaining the leaderhood status activates the ability to lead, and makes the person a leader-in-waiting (Externalised leadership that can be exhibited through holding a position or even without a position)
4. Latent leadership within that has become activated and applied can be enhanced through skills development and training. The quality of activated leadership can be enhanced.

THE TWO STATES OF LEADERSHIP

The Leadership Activation Perspective holds the view that Leadership as a natural human resource exists at two states:

- **Unactivated state**
- **Activated state**

Let us look at these two states:

Unactivated State: Latent Leadership Stage

Everyone has latent leadership in their natural systems of being. Leadership involves thoughts, awareness, concern and action, and everyone can think, become aware, can be concerned, and can take actions. At this unactivated state, leadership resides in the inner recess of a person, as a dormant natural resource, that requires activation. At this state, individuals possess "latent leadership", and are yet to attain leaderhood.

Activated State: Leaderhood Status

Leadership itself is not a process but involves some processes which begins with leaderhood.

Leaderhood is like puberty which is attained by certain natural processes. Puberty is time-based. When a person reaches a certain timeline, they attain puberty; a stage in life and a state of being, and that goes for leaderhood as well. Leaderhood is further comparable with maturity which is attained by the presence of certain factors. Maturity is a state of being, just like leaderhood.

Thoughts lead to the use of more initiatives for awareness, concern, and action, and these four activate the latent leadership within the person and brings a person to the attainment of leaderhood status.

The unactivated latent leadership in a person can become activated:
- Through thoughts and initiatives
- When they consciously become aware
- When they consciously become concerned
- When they consciously act about issues, or situations.

These four drivers of leadership: thoughts, awareness, concern, and action, could involve some processes.

At the point where a person's latent leadership becomes engaged by thoughts, conscious awareness, concern and action, latent leadership transforms into active mode, and leadership becomes activated. The attainment of the leadership activation stage leads such a person to act in different ways that position them as leaders, with or without official positions.

LEADERSHIP PROGRESSION

Leadership as an *internal* resource goes through some refining moments that take the individual leader through different phases of:

- Activation
- Application (opportunity to lead)
- Development (through further use of initiatives and reviewing previous experiences)
- Perfection (through the understanding of self and one's leadership circumstances; through *the* understanding of limitations and how to maximize achievements within those limitations.

Some factors could aid the occurrence or attainment of leadership activation, and these revolve around thoughtfulness, inquiry, and the use of initiative.

Influencing others to act is the 'action' part of 'leadership activation' and is just one aspect of leadership but Leadership is not only about the leader's actions. Although leading could and does involve actions targeted at influencing further actions, it starts from the intangible and progresses to the tangible. *Leading* starts from a stir of inward awareness and concern.

Individuals have desires and organisations think about achieving some goals which they usually refer to as their aims and objectives and these require performance. There could be several units of goals to be achieved and unless these different goals and desires are harmonized, personal or corporate efforts and resources could be wasted.

There is therefore the need to put together the several ideas and thoughts in a coherent way and that harmonization of ideas and thoughts can only be achieved through *careful thoughts,* awareness, concern and action. What makes possible the harmonization of goal achievement ideas is the innate resource within every human being and the Leadership Activation Perspective identifies that innate resource as "leadership".

Leadership is *to be viewed as that* innate resource *within everyone* that makes possible the harmonization of goal achievement *desires* through *thoughts,* awareness, concern, and action.

Leadership invariably involves the act of leading, however, distinct from leadership itself (as a noun) leading (a verb), has at least four parts and involves:
- thinking,
- information processing,
- analyzing facts
- performance

hence, we can talk of:

- Leadership Thoughts
- Leadership Research
- Leadership Analysis
- Leadership Practice (Application of the results of thoughts, research, and analysis)

Leading people involves thoughts, analysis, and actions and when people talk about leadership, they should not limit it to issues of performance or performance management.

The leader's thoughts and analysis would form the bulk of what can be described as 'Leadership conditioning', while the performance of the leader would be 'leadership practice'.

In leadership literature, most of what is written about leadership is about performance or achievement of goals and rightly falls under "Leadership practice", and no wonder, it is referred to as 'the process of attaining performance through influence'. However, before leaders can act, they first need to be able to think and analyze.

In literature, that part of leadership thought, and leadership analysis have not been adequately addressed by leadership scholars.

LEADERHOOD MAKES LEADING EFFECTIVE

The combination of leadership thoughts, analysis, and practice is what leadership activation represents and while each of these three could have processes, leadership itself is not a process as such, but the result of attaining leaderhood. The processes that lead to leaderhood, combine to transform a follower to a leader.

Leadership requires the use of initiatives, but this opens the question: how do you gauge the use of initiative? Instincts, hindsight, and innovation are important elements in the use of initiatives. What drives initiative? Several factors drive initiative and could include:

- Background
- Status
- Experience
- Knowledge

- Limitations (Existing/Non existing limitations affect how much initiative can be exercised). Limitations can be personal, systemic, *institutional,* or environmental.

And there could arise the need to find answers to many questions about the possession and use of initiatives by those who find themselves in leading positions. For example, do female initiative levels differ from male initiative levels? Whose level of initiative is higher? - Male of Female? Further research could help to determine how initiatives affect leadership activation and the act of leading.

Although Leadership practice is about leading, leadership is not synonymous with leading. Leadership, a human resource resident in everyone makes leading possible. Leading is the outward display of inner leadership. Most leadership literature describes 'leading' rather than leadership.

Leaderhood Theory, through the Leadership Activation Perspective focuses on leadership as a resource, (instrument) rather than as a synonym of leading and aims to show that leadership is universal and can be enhanced through levels of activation and that leadership activation leads to leadership practice. (Leading)

Leadership (as a noun that it is) is not a process, rather it involves a process.

LEADING IS THE PURPOSE OF LEADERSHIP

An individual could be in-charge without being a 'real leader'. In such cases, being in-charge is just a function of power and influence of that position. Such a person could better be described as a ruler, head, or coordinator rather than a leader. Ruling and leading are usually confused as leadership and relies on power and influence.

At this stage, there could be the need to distinguish between leading and leadership, *although some see them as interchangeable.* Leadership is individual and is the state of being that prepares a person for leading.

Different categories of people are often seen or referred to as leaders. Most managers are seen as leaders but are managers necessarily leaders? Heading a team or organisation is not necessarily leadership, though it reflects the "leading position" of such individuals.

Headship is the political aspect of managing people and though it has elements of leadership, headship does not fully define leadership. Power and authority reflect the political aspects of managing people rather than the leadership aspects. Not every position occupier or everyone with power and authority is a leader in the real sense of it. A leader is that person who has attained leaderhood by activating their leadership through thoughts, awareness, concern, and action.

In other words, to be a leader in the real sense of it, a person should first attain leaderhood by activating their leadership.

Those who see leadership as a process, focus on the use of power and influence as they see leadership itself as the outplay of power while influencing people for goals achievement.

However, should leadership be regarded as a process of influencing through power, it reduces leadership to the use of positional power for influential negotiations.
Is leadership strictly about power, influence, and goals? If that was the case, then leadership would amount to the process of influential negotiations based on positional power.

Viewing leadership as a process is one way of looking at leadership but there are alternative views (Yukl,2006) an example of which is 'the traits view of leadership' that shows leadership as strings of traits, special abilities and acumen possessed by special individuals who manage people, however, both the 'process definition' and the 'traits definition' do not fully explain the idea of leadership.

LEADERSHIP IS NOT ALL ABOUT INFLUENCE

Leadership is the God-given innate ability of all human beings but is activated at various levels in diverse ways. It is that innate ability, which when activated, propels the process of achieving results through influence.

Influence is not a one-way issue as it can be both vertical and horizontal. Those being led and those leading can have influence on the process of achieving goals.
(Kellerman, 2008; Xu et al., 2019; Northouse, 2019; Matthews et al.,2021)

Leading people could involve the use of influence, (Covey and Merrill, 2006; Kouzes and Posner, 2023) but the first person to be influenced is oneself. A person could influence himself to become *thoughtful, to become* aware, *to* become concerned and to act on issues and that is what triggers and activates the person's leadership.

Leading as distinct from leadership involves influencing people and consequently involves the possession and use of power. (Kotter, 1998; Northouse, 2010)

Some people occupy positions of power and authority over others based on their positions, training, and levels of influence.

Some have performed well in leading to the extent that they became reference points in the art and practice of leading, either because of their personalities, traits, conditions of birth, social standing, training, and other such factors.

On the other hand, some have not performed well in leading despite having enormous power and influence. This performance dichotomy has led to the debate on whether leaders are born or made.

2

ACTIVATING LEADERSHIP

THE 4 DRIVERS OF LEADERSHIP
Leadership is an innate virtue possessed by all but displayed by a few who have attained "leaderhood", which is a state of being, reached by an individual and transforms their dispositions from followers' dispositions to leaders' dispositions. Leaderhood precedes visible leadership abilities.

For a person to attain leaderhood status, the drivers of leadership need to be deployed. There are four drivers of leadership, and these are:
- **Thoughts: This is the leadership initiation stage**
- **Awareness: This is the information stage**
- **Concern: This is the analysis stage**
- **Action: This is the leadership activation stage**

Everything about leadership starts with thoughts. The thoughts level marks the beginning of leadership activation. At this stage, a person has active and deliberate thoughts about issues and their navigation. This state of thoughtfulness could be provoked by personal interest(self-influence), passion or challenge *(external influence)*.

Thoughtfulness initialises the process of leaderhood. When an individual reaches that point where they think *about*, experience, or show initial interest in *specific* issues, that individual has commenced a leadership journey. With the passage of time, every individual will reach that point in their work or non-work situations where they realise that issues involved are deeper than what they seem and give some thoughts to these issues. While these thoughts are on-going, leaderhood is being invoked.

Although every individual has it within them to work on the issues *in which they are involved*, some people would not be bothered, while some would go steps further to use their initiatives to navigate those situations by deploying their thoughts on such issues. *Such a person* thinks about what is, and what can be.

Without the drivers of leadership which are thoughts, awareness, concern and action, latent leadership would remain untapped. These leadership drivers play out as follows:

Thoughts:
Thoughts of leaders could involve considerations of goals set up, what goals are possible? and how to harmonize these possibilities.
To be a leader goes beyond just thinking about issues and the setting of goals. It further involves the deployment of leaderhood initiatives and that involves **"Thoughts, Awareness, Concern and Action."**

Awareness:
This includes intuition, comprehension, assimilation, investigation of these goal

achievement possibilities and their conditions (possibilities research)

Concern:
Applicable to both work and non-work issues, this includes analysis of pros and cons; identifying goal achievement pathways; result projections, and the analysis of possible effects of these conditions (Situational and Strategic analysis)

Action:
The leader's action could be to initiate new action or to orchestrate and catalyze processes. (Influence with or without power)

The "Process definition of Leadership" hangs leadership on the action part of leadership activation, but that is misconstrued as what leadership means in totality. Actions taken by individual leaders cannot become a template for all leaders because leadership is personal.

Leading in ideas, leading of people, or leading of processes starts from within and progresses into physical leading, eventually. Leaderhood is attained by the combination of the four leadership drivers of thoughts, awareness, concern, and action.

OFFICIAL POSITIONS AND LEADERSHIP ACTIVATION

Some people have not activated their leadership, and so, have not attained leaderhood status, but they find themselves in positions requiring them to lead. These sets of people are often seen as and called 'leaders' though in the real sense of it all they have is latent leadership, that everyone has.

These sets of people are positional leaders only and the positions they occupy stand in to fill the gap in their leadership activation. Such positional leaders rely on the authority and power vested in their positions. What they have is not activated leadership but mere demonstration of power. Some people who hold positions could better be described as coordinators or managers instead of being called leaders.

Positions usually come with power and positional power has been researched widely (Daft, 2005; Yukl,2006). Position is often confused with leadership, and it is common to interchange them, but this is not quite correct. People occupying official posts are in headship positions, and as such they are in **leading positions.** It is possible to be in headship positions without having leadership *activation in place, whereas leadership* is the activated innate ability to get results through thoughts, awareness, concern, and action.

A person needs to attain leaderhood (leadership *activation)* first and that qualifies them for positions requiring leadership. In essence, upon attaining leaderhood, the innate latent leadership is activated first and thereafter displayed. Everyone has latent leadership but those who have activated their leadership can become real leaders, with or without holding positions. To be a leader in the right use of the word, requires the possession and use of initiatives, ability to innovate and disrupt.

Leadership performance requires the display of the abilities to think, analyse and act appropriately in given situations.

LEADING WITHOUT ATTAINING LEADERHOOD

Is Leading without leadership activation possible?

There are clarifications to be made about leaders, leading and leadership.

It is important to note that not all those in leading positions have activated their leadership. Overseeing operations or teams could put a person in a leading position but that would not necessarily make him a real leader. He could be called a leader or seen as a leader but not in the real sense of it.

Leading with leaderhood in place, ensures presenting an agenda to people(followers) and getting them to follow the agenda presented to them. Getting people to do a task or complete a project is not necessarily 'leading' as that could be called ruling, directing or other names.

Those being 'led' in such cases are not real followers of a leader as they could only be following superior instructions because they have no better choices.

In the real sense of it, leading involves buy-in. When a person leads, it is important that those following instructions should appreciate the issues surrounding the instructions and possibly believe in what they are *being* led to do. There would have been some communications to exchange the leader's ideas or instructions with their acceptance and commitment. When that happens, there is buy-in, and such people would not only be obeying instructions, but they are following the 'leading' of a leader because they can see *or* appreciate his possession of leadership.

One question that could arise here is, "Is it possible to lead without Leadership activation"? Or put in another way, "Can a person that has not attained leaderhood, lead"?

Leading has to do with activities and being in charge involves coordination of activities. To that extent, it is possible to coordinate activities administratively without leadership activation. For example, an appointee could be in-charge and such an appointee could be someone without leadership activation. Some organisations could have the misfortune of placing people in charge even when they have not attained leaderhood and that could happen in societies, business or government. Such people usually do not meet up with general performance expectations.

What happens when someone leads without having leadership activation? Some people who head organisations are called leaders, but this is not to say that they all have leadership activation. Since leadership is a resource rather than a process, a real leader would have leadership activation in place, which enables the ability to *harness and apply thoughts, analysis and actions, for desired results.*

In some instances, some people, by virtue of their official positions as organisation heads, oversee others and rally them towards goals achievement. These set of organisational heads are better described as coordinators.

Coordinators of processes and activities could also be leaders if they have attained leaderhood and have activated their leadership. Some organisations have great administrators and top-level strategists and decision makers, and though they are also referred to as leaders, they would only be leaders, if they have *attained* leadership *activation*. Leadership, Management and Administration are not necessarily interchangeable.

It is possible to be the head of an organisation
- due to promotion into a higher office
- due to recognition of challenging work,
- due to political appointments
- due to nepotism, or any other consideration.

Headship does not necessarily translate to leadership. Headship is a function while leadership is a possession, and that makes it possible to head or try to lead without leadership.

Leading without leadership activation often leads to woeful results in the long-run because the efforts and activities become unsustainable due to lack of buy-in and lack of commitment.

In summary, it is possible to try leading without leadership, but it is impossible to lead well without leadership activation or leaderhood.

LEADERHOOD TRIGER
It has been mentioned severally that the innate ability called leadership is activated by four drivers: *thoughts,* awareness, concern, and action. Everyone is born with leadership abilities but not all exhibit that quality because they lack 'leadership activation' *until leaderhood is first attained and their latent leadership becomes activated.*

*T*he absence of any one of awareness, concern, and action, marks the absence of leadership activation rather than the absence of leadership ability.

People can be trained to attain leadership activation, and in that sense, they can be trained to be *active leaders*, but they were born as *latent leaders*, originally. Anyone that *has attained leaderhood would possess a level of* awareness of the situation; can show concern and can act, and such a person is a leader-in-waiting, even if he has no leadership position!

Incidence of leadership: Attaining Leaderhood status

As mentioned earlier, leadership is in everyone, however, until it is activated by the drivers of leadership, it remains dormant. Leadership that was erstwhile dormant and latent becomes alive through activation and that is the point of leadership incidence and that is when leaderhood status is attained.

Going past dormancy, when latent leadership becomes activated, it serves no practical use until it is applied to specific ideas or projects but there is a leader-in-waiting, ready and waiting for the opportunity to display his leadership.

There is a point at which there is the harmonisation of goal achievement *ideas*, through awareness, concern, and actions. The achievement of goals depends on quite a few factors but at the awareness stage, the *focus* is *on* the awareness of goals, awareness of issues around the goals and awareness about factors that could affect the achievement of such goals.

Beyond being aware of conditions and possibilities of goals achievement, the concern stage involves analysis of pros and cons, the consideration of pathways to achieving the set goals and the interrelatedness of issues that affect the goals.

Then comes the action stage which involves the charting of pathways for achieving the goals, *orchestrating,* and catalysing performance, and of course, actual performance, directly or through proxies.

THE TWO LEADERSHIP ACTIVATION ZONES

Leadership in each person can be activated to different levels or degrees and at different speeds or pace. Different people activate their leaderships differently and that creates *two* leadership activation zones as follows:

- **Leaders-** Those who have activated their leadership
- **Followers-** Those yet to activate or progress their leadership

Even for the leaders, because not all leaders activate their leaderships at the same level, two groups of leaders could emerge.

Some leaders have a high level of leadership activation while some leaders have a low level of leadership activation. It is like drinking alcohol.

A person who drank one cup cannot be on the same level of intoxication as another who drank three cups.

This difference in leadership activation among leaders create two groups of leaders:

- **Leaders among leaders (LAL)**
- **Followers among Leaders (FAL)**

Leaders with higher levels of leadership activation tend to emerge as leaders *in* the group of leaders. Other leaders look up to them for direction, guidance and support. These are Leaders Among Leaders (LAL)

What is the nature of Leaders Among Leaders? How do they emerge as leaders of other leaders? Some Scholars believe and Literature suggests that some people have some special endowments and personality or power that make them exceptional leaders. (Houpt et al., 2015).

However, according to 'Leaderhood Theory', it is not their personalities that distinguish them but their higher level of leadership activation. In other words, they have deployed more awareness, more concern, and more action.

The Followers Among Leaders (FAL) are also leaders in their own rights and individually they could be excellent people and resources managers. However, their level of leadership activation is comparatively lower than the Leaders Among Leaders and therefore commensurate to their level of leadership activation, they would be Followers Among Leaders. Therefore, we find leaders among leaders as well as followers among leaders.

CAUSES OF LEADERSHIP TUSSLES
Why do leadership tussles occur? There could be several reasons for leadership tussles but in terms of Leadership Activation, Leadership tussles occur when two or more Leaders Among Leaders have comparable high levels of leadership activation.

Each of these leaders with high leadership activation qualifies to be Leader Among Leaders, and that leads to some clashes of activation. Hardly does Leadership tussles occur in the group of Followers Among Leaders.

When leaders are of equal level of leadership activation, submission becomes almost impossible among them and this could be due to ego, negative peer influence and acceptability. It also becomes difficult for equals to submit to one another due to political ratings, *possibly because* submitting to an equal could affect the ratings of the submitting leader, who could now be seen as inferior.

Fallout of submission also make it difficult for leaders to submit to one another *probably because* submitting to an equal, could diminish legitimacy, especially in power-driven leading situations, like in Politics, for example.

Among leaders therefore, mostly, those who emerge as Leaders Among Leaders are those whose levels of leadership activation have evidently advanced beyond their peers. Advancing one's leadership activation level could be intentional and it could be intense. For some people leadership activation is casual.

Leadership activation occurs *generally,* at two points:

- The Internal Realm
- The External Realm

Of the *four* drivers of leadership, t*hree* drivers of leadership: *thoughts,* awareness, and concern, take place first internally, while the *fourth* driver (Action)takes place externally. *People only see the application of the fourth driver, (action) but it all started internally, within the individual.* Leadership activation becomes visible at the point of action, but it started with ideation, awareness of issues, concerns about status quo, concerns about gaps and analysis of possibilities. The *final* leg of the leadership driver, (action), finalizes the activation of leadership and this is the external part of leadership activation.

A person can think like a leader or analyze like a leader but until he acts like a leader, his leadership activation is incomplete. How do leaders act?

Leaders act on issues they have thought on and analyzed with concern. Leadership activation, therefore, is the action-based externalization of internal awareness, concern, and analysis, of issues and situations.

Leadership does not start or end with leadership action and what a leader does is based on thoughts, initiatives, analysis, and performance.

TYPES OF LEADERSHIP ACTIVATION

Different people activate their leaderships at different paces as follows:

Mechanical activation:

- Some people experience slow-paced mechanical activation based on deliberate well-thought-out deep thinking. This kind of activation has a logical flow.

Brainwave Activation:

- Some other people experience spontaneous brainwave activation based on spur of the moment. Such people have ideas, and they think briefly and then act. The level of analysis is not necessarily shallow, but not deep.

Riotous Activation:

- Some people experience ad-hoc riotous activation that is nonspecific. This kind of activation is open, on-going and situational. Such people base their actions on convergence of ideas and events without any specific pattern.

Leadership activation can either be casual or intense and it is not uncommon for Leaders Among Leaders (LAL) to experience intense leadership activation while Leaders Among Followers experience (LAF) experience casual leadership activation. The difference between the two is the intensity of thought, analysis and action needed in each case. The level of responsibility needed could also be instructive to dictate the level of casualness or intensity needed in leadership activation.

STAGES OF LEADERSHIP ACTIVATION
Leadership activation can pass through different stages as follows:
- Dormant stage
- Activation stage
- Application stage
- Development stage
- Perfection stage

Let us look at these *stages* in turn:
- **Dormant stage**
  Everyone is born with leadership instincts but at this stage it is not refined and unused. It is dormant and may not even be recognisable. This is the latent leadership stage.

- **Activation stage**
  When a person engages the *four* drivers of leadership activation by *thinking,* showing awareness, concern, and action, about an issue, process, condition or practice, the latent leadership within becomes turned on and at this stage there is a leader-in-waiting.

- **Application stage**
  When a person has activated his leadership through the drivers, he needs to put his leadership to contextual use. Sometimes what people need is the opportunity to show their leadership. This stage is marked by being visibly in-charge

- **Development stage**
  Leadership activation is repeatable over time. Once a person has become aware, concerned, and has acted, such a person can continue to get more awareness, be more concerned and take more action. Through these repeat-activations, *the* person's leadership *potential and capabilities* grow and develop but what develops is not leadership resource but leadership acumen. This stage could *involve the* reviewing of previous levels of activation and their adjustments.

- **Perfection stage**
  When a person has activated their leadership and has applied that

activation over time, some experiences are gained and that leads to the understanding of self- leadership abilities. At this stage, a leader clearly understands his limitations as a leader, having developed his leadership over time. At this stage, the leader's leadership attains perfection, and he understands what he can do or *unable* to do to maximise achievements within those limitations.

With further exposure to leadership actions, a leader passes from *being* some unknown person to an adored leader. Leadership perfection could take time and it is continuous. However, when a person's leadership perfection is not properly matched by leadership responsibilities, it could lead to negative results.

3

LEADING AND LEADERSHIP

LEADING VS LEADERSHIP

Is leading the same as leadership? Granted that leadership is a resource rather than the process of influencing performance, what is generally described as leadership in literature is "leading" (the leaders' actions) and quite distinct from leadership resource.

Apart from the grammatical classification of "leading" as a verb and "leadership" as a noun, leading is not the same as leadership and most of the confusion in understanding leadership has come from not being able to distinguish leading from leadership.

- Among other things, leading involves:
- An understanding of frameworks (Conventions)
- An understanding of requirements (Aims, Objectives, Visions)
- An understanding of the environment (Limitations)

- The ability to match requirements with provisions.
- The ability to identify gaps in provision
- The ability to identify how to close the provision gap
- The ability to communicate the gaps in provision and performances
- The ability to guide the gap-bridging
- The ability to include and involve stakeholders in gap-bridging
- The ability to review the performance of the gap-bridging exercise

In summary, leading is the ability to influence performance through:

- Identification of performance requirements
- Communicating the gaps in requirements and provision
- Inclusion and involvement of others in the planning, execution, and review of gap-bridging activities, with the focus on meeting agreed or specified aims and objectives. Leading is leadership in action and most of the literature on

leadership is about leading or what can be called "Leadership practice".

LEADERSHIP CYCLE

Leading is the essence of attaining leaderhood and the activation of latent leadership. Every aspect that leads up to the application of leadership resources can be represented by the leadership cycle. At the centre of the leadership cycle is the **leading function**.

The leadership cycle commences with a review of situations in the mind of the potential leader and that engages the God-given latent leadership.

With the drivers of leadership (thoughts, awareness, concern and action) being fully applied to latent leadership, leaderhood is attained. This is the process of initial leadership activation.

Leaderhood is attained through thoughts and with intentional awareness, concern, and action, that latent leadership becomes activated, **(leadership activation).**

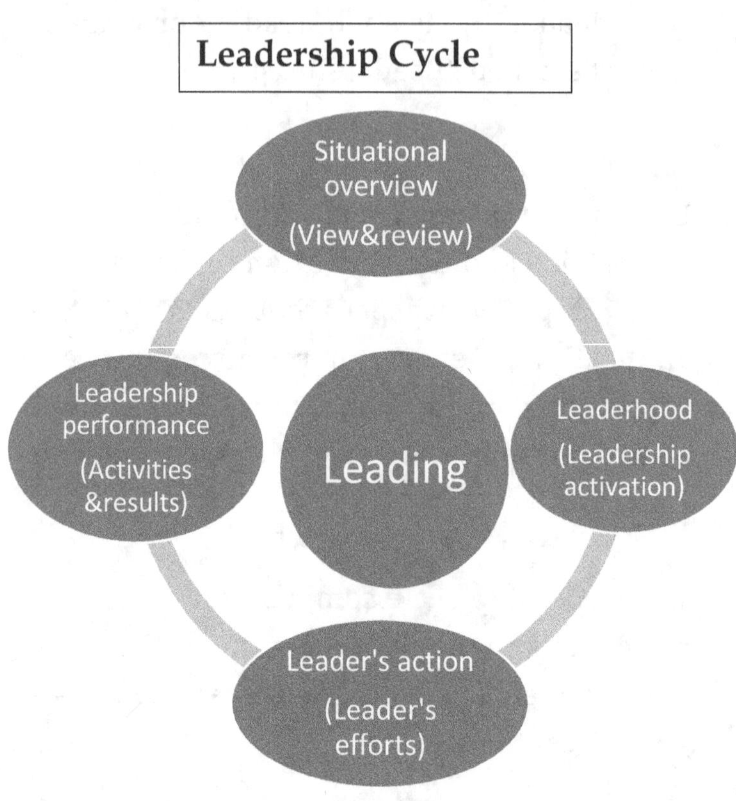

© Felix Asade

When such individuals get the opportunity to occupy leading positions, they act as leaders **(leadership action)** and those actions lead to performance **(leadership performance).**

Leadership performance become reviewed with feedbacks and leads to more awareness, more concern and more action and the cycle continues until leadership maturity is attained.

From the leadership cycle, it is understood that the cycle can be repeated over, and over and greater levels of leadership activation are possible.

NON-POSITIONAL LEADING

The idea and scope of leadership is both tangible and intangible. Most times, people focus only on "Tangible Leadership" and "Tangible Followership", by emphasising physical positions, offices, and titles.

Some literature on types of leaders have focused on the traits of leaders or their styles of operation and this emphasises physical or tangible leadership, whereas leadership is a compound natural gift with diverse resources within it and these resources include thinking, analysis and performance. Leadership is not just about positions and the actions of those in positions.

When we look at leadership as a state of being (leaderhood) measured by activation levels, we move away from classifications of leaders based on traits or styles and we focus on practicalities.

Although leadership is innate and owned by all, the level of leadership activation differs, and the leadership route also differs. Leadership route specifies the areas where leadership could be proved and *applied, and these* include Thoughts, Processes and Practice.

A leader could therefore be a:
- Leader of Thoughts
- Leader of Processes
- Leader of Practice

Individuals are gifted differently and because leadership is individual, there is the possibility that everyone would not have the same focus of leadership activation and the route of leadership activation could also differ equally.

Some people could activate their leadership in the "Thoughts Arena", some others could activate their leadership in the "Process Arena" and some others could activate their leaderships at the "Practice Arena".

Whichever route of leadership, *they* all require activation through the drivers of leadership, that is, thoughts, awareness, concern and action.

Is it possible for an individual to activate the three leadership routes of Thoughts, Processes and Practice? Some leaders have moved from one route to another in a circular manner while it is difficult to pin some leaders down to specific leadership route because they have activated all, at different times.

More people would be recognised as leaders if the measurement is based on leadership route activation, rather than on headship, administration, or positions. Some people are very good at thinking because they have activated that aspect of leadership.

Some are very good in processes because
they have activated that aspect of leadership.
Yet, some are very good with actual Practice
because that is what they have activated
within their stock of leadership resources.

IN PRACTICE
Leaders of Thoughts:
Clearly, leaders of thoughts focus more on
ideas. Such a person has innate abilities to
think comprehensively and comparatively.
They can convey their thoughts convincingly.

A leader of thoughts would be that person
who has:

- **Awareness** of current situations, awareness of possibilities, awareness of limiting factors
- **Concern** for the identified gaps, concern for achieving betterments, concern for how to make it happen, concern for pros and cons,
- **Action:** A common action taken by leaders of thoughts is communicating and broadcasting their thoughts *and* lobbying support for their ideas

—

Leaders of thoughts seem to have inexhaustible ideas and they are good with research. They investigate and analyse, and they convey their findings. Leaders of thoughts may not function so well in moving processes and operations, but they are reservoir of thoughts and thoughtfulness.

Leaders of thoughts tend to generally have a high level of awareness and the propensity for investigations, research and fact finding. Sometimes their ideas could look erratic or illogical but could hold the key to better processes and performances. Leaders of thoughts could be good with strategy formulation.

Leaders of Processes

Leaders of Processes are those people who focus more on methods, operational procedures, and technicalities. These are mechanical in nature. Leaders of Processes are usually analytical, mathematical, and calculative. They are good with ensuring operational flow. These could make good Project Mangers, Legislators, Lawyers, Teachers.

Leaders of Practice

Leaders of Practice are those who focus on operational performance. They understand what the targets are and work towards achieving such targets. These could be Administrators, Managers, Teachers.

Some people could be a combination of leaders of thoughts, processes, and practice but it is uncommon. Even when that happens, they will tilt to one than the other. Either they are great at planning and deficient in actions or great with implementations and deficient with ideas generation. A good mix of these diverse types of leaders will position an organisation for success and sustainability.

4

MANAGEMENT AND LEADERSHIP

MANAGER OR LEADER?

There is the need to understand the relationship between managing and leading. It is managing and leading that can be compared rather than comparing management and leadership. Managing involves coordinating and controlling resources, people, and their activities, through set rules.

Managing could involve the engagement of individuals using initiatives, innovation, and performance, to coordinate and guide individuals and this is synonymous with leading.

In general terms, Management involves planning, coordination, and control, (Cole and Kelly,2015) but it also has a leadership aspect which is accentuated by the *four* drivers of leadership:

- Thoughts
- Awareness
- Concern
- Action

When these four drivers of leadership are combined, leadership activation occurs and leaderhood is attained by that individual regardless of whether he is called a manager or a leader. Managing or leading people efficiently requires thoughts and the understanding of the use of awareness, concern and action, and that understanding is the leadership aspect of managing people.

How much of leadership is offered by people managers? It would be incorrect to give a blanket classification that managers are different from leaders or to say that managers are not leaders.

Whether people managers simply manage, or they lead, would depend on their levels of leadership activation and that would be a function of their levels of thoughts, awareness, concern and action.

Leadership is a possession (leaderhood), that qualifies a person for leading and sometimes it is visible and at other times it is not visible. Leadership displayed is visible leadership and is the more usual form of leading people. Leadership activation could have been reached by an individual but if such an individual has no platform to display their leadership, it would be there but invisible.

Some people's leadership is passive yet effective. That is, they can be aware, they can be concerned and act behind the scenes. Such people do not have the titles of leaders on them, or they are not known as leaders, yet they make things happen due to their enormous influences. People look up to them although such people may not hold any official position.

A simple "Leadership-Driver-Analysis" could be instructive in determining if a person in-charge is a manager or a leader and that analysis could play out as follows:

Thoughts: What is the level of thoughts involved or required? Some situations, especially work situations does not require much thought because there are rules already in place. A person who is required to coordinate others by just following rules is more likely a manager. Getting others to work according to set rules is not leadership but it could still be called "leading". Leading involves a greater level of thinking about the issues and the people while managing can be a matter of just routing for compliance.

Awareness: What is the level of awareness of people managers in terms of their:

- Awareness of issues
- Awareness of timing
- Awareness of performance possibilities
- Awareness of contradictions
- Awareness of frictional possibilities

Concern: What is the level of concern of people managers in terms of their:

- Concern for form, substance, structure
- Concern for goals achievement
- Concern for procedural attainments
- Concern for individuality
- *Concern for issues resolution*

Action*:* What is the level of action of people managers towards goals attainment? It is common for people managers to focus their actions on performance, but do they consider the value of other peoples' actions?

These considerations of the level of *thoughts,* awareness, concern, and action of people managers, mark their leadership abilities rather than just a broad or general distinction between management and leadership.

Literature suggests vast differences between management and leadership and there is the trend of discussions seeking to separate management from leadership (Rost, 1993; Kotterman,2006; Kotter, 2008; Bush, 2020) but a manager can also be a leader, if such a manager has attained leaderhood.

Goals attainment is the objective of management. Leadership, as presented to be a process of influencing people towards goals attainment is quite like management and seems to make goal performance the destination or aim of leadership. And to that extent, both management and leadership have the same endpoint, which is goals performance. However, can it be correct to assume that leadership is a series of activities leading to goal performance?

The process of influencing people to achieve set-goals could at best be a description of one element of leadership activation, which is: "taking action", and that could involve negotiating and influencing performance, but taking action is not all what leadership is. The 'process definition of leadership' describes "leading" or "leadership action", rather than leadership itself.

Those who coordinate the efforts of people towards set standards are usually found in the business context and these are called managers, since they manage all business resources at their disposal. It is also possible to have variations of management in family units, workplaces, Faith centres, and in the nation. In essence there could be private managers and institutional managers, for example:

- Family managers (husband and wife) would be private managers. They head their mini organisation called the family and supply guidance and leadership services in the home.
- Workplace Managers (team leaders, supervisors, and managers) could be either private or public, depending on circumstances.
- Faith Centre Managers (Pastors, Imams, and other titles). These head their spiritual organisations and supply guidance and leadership services to their congregations.
- Societal Managers could span private organisations through to national organisations. Incorporated

Associations could have Boards of
Managers or Directors, there could be
parastatal heads as well as other
national managers. The Mayors,
Governors, Prime-Ministers, and
Presidents are Public Managers as
well.

Any of these involved in managing people in
families, workplaces, faith centres or in the
society, can be leaders if they activate their
leaderships and attain leaderhood. Without
leaderhood, such people are best described as
rulers, heads, or coordinators.

**IS MANAGEMENT DIFFERENT FROM
LEADERSHIP?**
Is striving to distinguish between
management and leadership necessary?
These distinctions pitch one against the
other creating a Management versus
Leadership explanations. If Leadership were
to be a process, such a comparison could be
justifiable, but management is a process
while leadership is an ability, hence both are
incomparable.

Scholars opined that leaders and managers differ in many respects. (Zalenik, 1977; Rost, 1993; Mintzberg, 1998; Rowe, 2001; Kotterman, 2006; Kotter, 2008; Bush, 2020). Zalenik (1977) asserted that an individual cannot be a manager and leader at the same time, but this view is challengeable because Managers who have attained leaderhood are also leaders!

Mintzberg (1998) separated leaders and managers based on their focus. Generally, Management is said to be interested in operations while leadership is said to be interested in direction and empowerment. This view still segregates management from leadership. *Those* who are in-charge or those who hold *management* positions are generally referred to as "the leadership", and they are leaders, *if they have activated their leadership.*

Those in management *could fall into one of the three categories of* leaders *of thoughts, leaders of processes or leaders of practice* and they are concerned with getting things done according to set goals.

In general terms, Mangers are basically "leaders of practice", *and it would be incorrect to say they are not leaders.* They are geared towards achieving specific organisational goals and their focus is on results. Managers, as individuals activate their leadership around performance. They deploy the drivers of leadership towards performance and concentrate on:

- **Awareness of performance requirements:**

This can be about tasks performance, operational performance, or general strategic performance

- **Concern for meeting performance goals:**

This can be about efficient use of resources for goals performance

- **Actions relating to performance**

It should be noted that Management and Leadership cannot be compared. It is Managing and Leading that can be compared.

Leadership is also different from "The Leadership". While leadership is individual, "the leadership" is used to describe those in headship, collectively.

LEADERSHIP ASPECTS OF PEOPLE MANAGEMENT

When the leadership aspects of managing people are discountenanced, the whole exercise of leading people becomes mere exercise of official controls on people, and that could have negative impacts on morale, productivity, and performance.

People operate and work in different settings and under different conditions and circumstances. It is not unusual to find a group of people being led by one or more people. Whether these people come together for business, recreation, or work, their operations and actions must be properly harnessed and coordinated by those who lead such groups or businesses. In that regard, we can talk of "people management".

People management would therefore refer to how people are coordinated when they engage in activities, and this can be in:

- Families- As Family members
- Workplaces- As (1) Individuals (2) Teams (3) Workforce
- Worship centres – As people of Faiths
- Society – As citizens

To manage people is to manage what they do. In Business, people are part of general business resources made up of Man, Machines, Money and Materials. Without Man (People who work), there can be no business. People are attracted and employed to complete the resources needed to produce value in a business.

Without people:

- Money would be in the bank and at best get interest
- Machine will not work by itself
- Material will never be transformed into products

Without people, no value can be created. The effort of man synergises and synchronises the values in money, machines, and materials to produce better and increased overall value for the organisation. Value is added by human resources.

As useful as man is in creating and keeping in business, if man is not effectively 'managed' there could be issues of clashes between Individual Personalities of the people and the Corporate Goals of the organisation. In work situations especially, man needs to be 'managed' to standardise efforts towards agreed performance and this is achieved by planning, coordination, and control, which is otherwise known as management. Business activities and roles are coordinated using corporate set-objectives as control standard.

One important question that requires to be answered is in relation to what exactly is to be managed in people. In other words, what is to be managed when people are led in an organisation? The aspirations, goals and efforts of people need to be managed as well as their dispositions.

In general terms, in people management, the
following needs to be managed:
- Ideas
- Skills
- Inputs, efforts, performances
- Lack of interest(apathy)
- Lack of motivation
- Personalities (Blending of cultures:
  individual culture needs to be blended
  with the corporate culture.

These efforts towards managing the above
requires leadership.

People are supposed to be led rather than
being managed. There are aspects of leading
that are psychological and could involve the
application of theories of motivation or
rewards. There are other aspects of
managing people that requires more than
coordination and control.

One error would be to treat human beings the
same way as other business resources would
be treated because people have emotions and
personalities.

'Managing people' requires leadership, especially the aspect that requires the management of cultures. The people manager should be able to lead individuals and groups to achieve culture blending. This could involve mentoring, and coaching. This is the use of leadership to navigate inevitable bends and smoothen rough edges of cultural contradictions.

Everyone could have their personal idiosyncrasies and these being different from the corporate culture, presents cultural contradictions which needs to be eased off from time to time, until cultural alignment is achieved. Business managers do not have the time to do that. They have their performance targets, and they can care less about cultural alignment, if performance is achieved. This is one reason that make theorists to believe that Management and Leadership are different. And there are countless differences put forward. (Kotter, 1990)

Achieving cultural alignment and business performance are not mutually exclusive. A manager can be a leader if he possesses leadership activation. Managers lead people but that does not automatically mean they have attained leaderhood.

As mentioned earlier, there is a difference between leading and leadership. Managing is like leading and could be procedural while leadership is a state of being of an individual whether he is managing people or being managed by others.

In managing people, the aim of the leadership (those in headship) should be the continuous generation of more leaders through the proliferation of leadership activation among the people being managed. In the home, the aim of parents as leaders should be to support their children to attain greater levels of awareness, concern and action towards the achievement of their set goals.

At work, the aim of the people managers (team leaders, Supervisors, Managers) should
be how to support workers to attain goal performance on one side, and to become leaders in their own rights as well.

Leading people at work is a double-edged leadership effort to:
- Achieve the organisation's goals
- Grow leadership potentials of the people.

Both leaders and followers have leadership abilities at different levels and so when we look at the leadership aspects of managing people we should also look at:
- Leadership aspects in relation to leaders
- Leadership aspects in relation to followers

People management has people on both sides:
- People being managed- (Followers)
- People managing them- (Leaders)

Realising that both leaders and followers have impact in the issues relating to leading will help to understand what the leadership considerations and issues are for both the followership(followers) and the leadership (those leading).

In essence, the leadership aspect of people management is the understanding of the processes and mix of values that lead to the activation of leadership of the people we manage or head.

THE LEADERS' AIMS
The aim of the leadership should not be only about goals performance but also to bring out the leadership potentials in people being managed. It involves any and every effort towards making people aware, concerned and active.

For those who manage other people, they need to develop and show their awareness, concern and action about issues affecting the people they look to coordinate and control.

In the society, the aim of leadership should be how to support citizens to achieve national performance goals and how citizens develop their own leadership. At the society level 'the leadership' should focus on transforming the citizens from followers to leaders and that can be achieved through:

- Orientations
- Instructions (via legislations)
- Participations and Involvement

Leadership aspects of people management also involve the exchange of influences between leaders and followers. Followers have influence among themselves, on the system, on their leaders and on the public at large.

Leadership is not only about the leaders, and it should be clarified that real leadership is not about rulership.

Managing people effectively requires the understanding of people, understanding their idiosyncrasies, and understanding their peculiarities.

People have different personalities, and the management of people can better be done by understanding these peculiarities.

Organisations and institutions formulate rules targeted at harmonising the behaviours of these otherwise diverse personalities through institutional policies and procedures. These policies guide behaviour and work in the society.

For too long, focus of people management in organisations has been on how to use rules, procedures, and policies to guide corporate behaviour, for the attainment of corporate goals, whatever these are. It is however doubtful if many people managers understand that the management of people goes beyond the use of rules and policies.

The management of people at whatever location, unit or group has various aspects like legal, social, professional, political and leadership aspects.

Often, the leadership aspects of people management are either neglected or misunderstood and this could be because of an inadequate or incorrect understanding of what leadership is about.

Management is vast and includes leading people at many fronts and that is why it is important to look at the leadership aspects of managing people.

Are the rules the same or different between managing people in private and public institutions? The rules of engagement in private institutions could vary and differ from the rules of engagement in managing public institutions but the common denominator is people, and people must be led effectively for satisfactory results to be achieved.

5

LEADERSHIP GROWTH

&

DEVELOPMENT

IS LEADERSHIP DEVELOPMENT POSSIBLE?

In general terms what is commonly referred to as leadership development revolves around skills upgrading for those in leading positions so that they can become more effective at leading. That is premised on the presumption that leadership is either a set of activities or set of skills or a combination of both. However, the idea of skills upgrading (in the name of leadership development) refers to leading, not leadership.

While physical leadership ability can increase, leadership is not taught.
What is taught is how people can activate and grow the activation of their God-given innate leadership.

—

78

In essence, people can learn how to improve their use of that latent leadership resource within them.

Leadership as an innate resource can be activated *and enriched* but cannot be grown. *Contrary to what some people believe,* leadership is not a skill set and cannot be taught or *learned. However, leading skills can be taught.* Leaderhood is attained when that inner resource becomes activated through awareness, concern, and action. At that point, latent leadership (innate ability to lead) becomes ready to be utilized in actual leading.

People can be trained to become aware of their leadership potentials and how to activate their leadership. When a person has activated his leadership, such a person becomes ready to lead and can then be trained in how to lead effectively. What he is taught is "leading" not leadership. Leading is a skill while leadership is a resource.

CAN LEADERSHIP GROW?

Can leadership grow or be developed? It is doubtful if leadership as a resource can be increased but the application of that resource can be extended.

Consider leadership to be like a piece of elastic band that is within each human being. That elastic band can be stretched, and its eventual length would be dependent on the level of force applied to stretching it. If stretched a little, the length would be as much and if stretched much, the length would be according to the stretch.

The forces applied to stretch that 'elastic band' are the *four* drivers of leadership: *thoughts,* awareness, concern, and action. Just as that elastic band can be stretched but its original length cannot be increased, so also is it with leadership as a resource. The application of leadership can increase but leadership itself does not change.

The level of leadership, therefore, shown by an individual will reflect the level of his *thinking,* awareness, concern, and action. More *thinking, more* awareness, more concern, and more action, would activate leadership further and stretch the 'leadership elastic' to a greater length, as it were. When a person gets more aware; becomes more concerned and takes more action, his leadership capacity will expand and that is leadership development.

When a person learns skills of leading effectively, that is *'leading skill development'* rather than leadership development. Leadership development can occur with more leadership activation. The innate resource does not necessarily increase rather it is the use of that resource that can be increased. As leadership ability is used increasingly, the leadership ability of such a person grows.

CAN LEADERSHIP GROWTH BE MEASURED?

It should be possible for an individual to gauge his own leadership and figure out if his ability has grown.

One key feature of leadership growth is experience. The more a person utilizes his leadership, the more "leadership experience" he gets and the more his leadership capacity expands.

Leadership activation can be elasticized by intense awareness, intense concern, and intense action.

Leadership growth or leadership development refers to the expansion of leadership use *(application)* rather than the growth of leadership itself, which is a resource.

A person who wants to develop his leadership should:
- Activate leadership
- Apply leadership
- Increase leadership activation
- Apply the increased activation

When a person expands his leadership activation, such a person would have moved across at least four leadership zones:

- Latency
- Activation
- Development
- Maturity

If leadership grows, it is from inactive status (latent leadership) to activated status(leaderhood) through the drivers of leadership (*thoughts*, awareness, concern, and action). At the activated status level, the leadership ability of a person becomes obvious. Leadership usage leads to development of greater leadership capacity and with more usage and experience, leadership maturity sets in.

6

LEADERS' BEHAVIOUR

BEHAVIOUR OF LEADERS OR LEADERSHIP BEHAVIOUR?

Most of what some people classify as leadership behaviour is mere documentation of the habits of some office holders. Many office holders have shown researchable dispositions while exercising the power of their offices and these sometimes-arbitrary dispositions have been relied upon as some regular traits of leaders.

Not everyone holding an office would always behave in the same way and it would be incorrect to use sample behaviours of a few to specify leadership traits. The behaviours of office holders would still be their behaviours even if they did not hold positions. Why such behaviours are noticed is because they are visible people because of their positions. Their individual behaviours cannot be a prescription of how leaders should behave.

Since leadership itself is individual, it has no specific behaviour. The nature of leadership can be described rather than the behaviour of leadership. The idea of leadership behaviour suggests that leadership is systemic.

Although the term "the leadership" is used to describe a group of leaders in an organization, leaders are individuals with leadership abilities that vary in depth, scope, activation and usage. The plurality of leaders and their differing levels of activation makes it difficult or impossible to be categorized homogeneously.

Leaders' actions could have systemic ramifications. Some leaders' actions are based on their positional powers and the authority attached to their offices. In such instances, their actions tend to permeate every stratum of that organization and because of that, *such* leaders' actions or behaviours could be systemic.
And this is possibly one reason there is confusion about leadership because systemic leaders' actions are misconstrued as what leadership is all about.

Thus, models built on studying leaders' behaviours in this kind of systemic situation would misrepresent how all leaders behave or how they are meant to behave. This 'systemic leadership' idea paints leadership behaviour as being homogeneous while it is not, and gives the wrong impression that leadership is also systemic and predictable.

In practice, while leadership activation is systematic because it rallies around awareness, concern and action, leadership itself is individual and not systemic. Attempts to systematize leadership have resulted in its being described as a process and has robbed away the actual meaning of leadership. Leadership practice can be a process, however.

DO LEADERS BEHAVE THE SAME WAY?
Broad classifications of leaders' behaviours are possible, but such broad categorizations cannot be safely specified as recurrent behaviour of leaders in general.

This is partly because behaviour of individual leaders could depend on many distinct factors including culture, background, dispositions, and experience.

A leader who came from a blame culture would lead differently to a leader from a praise culture. A blame culture is where faults are magnified rather than the solution and someone must be the scapegoat and gets punished. Leaders from such a culture will possibly be highhanded and punitive. On the other hand, a praise culture is that which magnifies what has been achieved and works towards achieving whatever gaps that exist. Leaders from a praise culture would be encouraging and not be fault finders.

As different leaders behave differently according to their leadership activation statuses, it is doubtful if there can be an umbrella theory to explain "leadership behaviour", however, leaders' behaviours can be explained.

Leaders behave according to the levels of their leadership activation.

As stated earlier, leaders can develop their activation across the four zones of: Latency, Activation, Development and Maturity. The behaviours of leaders could differ *at* these four leadership activation zones.

- **Leaders' Behaviour at Latency**

At this stage the individual only has latent or dormant leadership, and the drivers of leadership (*thoughts,* awareness, concern, and action) are either non-existent or carelessly handled.

At this stage, such an individual would only be a follower. At this stage such an individual, though full of potential to lead, would not be interested in what is going on around him. Such individuals would be satisfied to follow others and just do as they are told. Even when issues arise, such an individual would be indifferent if his own rights are not impinged upon.

At this stage, such an individual is only interested in himself and cares less about the organisation or society. Such an individual would be a "Follower Among Followers".

- **Leaders' Behaviour at Activation**

When a "Follower Among Followers" begin to show awareness of situations and becomes concerned about the state of things, such a person has triggered the process of becoming a leader. At this stage, such individual sees more than his selfish position. Such an individual begins to ask questions about what is going on or why things are like they are. Eventually this individual could take some actions about issues on hand. Even if such actions are min*imal*, it finalises the activation stage and sets that individual up as a "Leader Among Followers".

At this stage, such an individual takes it upon himself to ensure that things go well. Leaderhood status is attained at that point and such a person thinks and acts like a leader, even if he does not hold any visible leading position.

- **Leaders' Behaviour at Development**

When opportunity to lead avails, the individual who has activated his leadership through thoughts, awareness, concern and action would be ready to lead and attain good performance.

While leading, such individual will need to exercise more awareness, more concern and more action, and this expands his activation and improves how he leads. At this stage, the leadership *practice* of such an individual grows by application and such an individual gains more insight into the workings of the system and the organisation. At this stage, such a leader masters his game and leads with precision.

- **Leaders' Behaviour at Maturity**

Having developed his leadership by practice, such a leader becomes a father-figure (patriarch) or mother-figure(matriarch) in the organisation.

At this level, the leader exhibits greater awareness, greater concern and takes far reaching decisions.

At such a stage the leader becomes like a coach and mentors others. At this stage such an individual will likely be a "Leader Among Leaders" and cannot be easily ignored without negative repercussions to the organisation.

COMMUNICATING AS A LEADER

Regardless of the level of leading opportunity open to a leader, one sure gauge of his behaviour as leader, is his communication ability.

Granted that leadership is a resource and cannot be taught, and granted that leading skills can be taught, a vital aspect of a leader's skill that can be taught is the ability to communicate appropriately. How leaders communicate reflects their behaviour.

What is to be communicated? Some of the things that a leader might wish to communicate can be his thoughts, processes, and performances.

"Thoughts communication": could include the following:

- Ideas
- Aims
- Objectives

"Processes Communication": could include the following:

- Procedures
- Policies

"Performance Communication": could include the following:

- Performance targets
- Performance paths
- Performance obstacles
- Performance achievements
- Performance gaps
- Performance failure

A leader could wish to communicate his delight or disgust in terms of thoughts, processes, and performances. It is not what is communicated that is the issue but how it is communicated.

And how people communicate differs from one person to the other.

How people communicate could depend on the culture they came from or subscribe to. Two distinct cultures are: Culture of Praise and Culture of Blame.

Communication as a leader occurs at different level:

- Communicating with followers
- Communicating with leaders
- Communicating with Stakeholders: This can include private and public entities or society at large

There are two distinct ways to communicate, either by command or by request. A leader can tell his followers what to do or involve them in deciding what to do. A leader can either tell the followers what to do or sell his ideas to them. When a leader sells his ideas to the followers, he can expect the followers to "buy-in" into his ideas.

The level of the audience usually decides the way to communicate with them.

For example, when communicating with leaders, it is not expected to "tell" them, rather one is expected to "sell" ideas to them and expect buy-in. And it could be useful also to avoid "telling" followers, depending, of course, on the level of their understanding of issues at stake. Sometimes it is proper to tell and sometimes it is not. A good leader would know when to tell and when to sell.

What else does a leader communicate? A leader could communicate his pleasures or his frustrations:

- Pleasures- could be in terms of personal, team and organizational achievements
- Frustrations- could be in the areas of how followers have been following or how the environment /stakeholders have been frustrating the leader and his efforts.

How a leader with leadership activation would communicate would be different from a leader without leadership activation. The leader with leadership activation will most likely communicate in a way to ginger the followers to become aware; to become concerned and to act.

Communication by leaders with leadership activation leads to performance, through further leadership activation of the followers. That is, goals performance become achieved by ensuring that followers get awareness and become part of the processes and actions.

Leaders with leadership activation therefore achieve two things:
- Leadership activation of their followers
- Goals performance

Leaders with leadership activation perpetuate performance and the leadership activation of their followers.

Communication by leaders without leadership activation produces only performance.

Leaders without leadership activation perpetuate:
- Followership
- Dependence on the leader
- Dependence on the system

7

LEADING POLITICS

ARE LEADERS BORN OR MADE?
The Politics of leadership includes the consideration of issues relating to the emergence of leaders, power of leaders and the leader-follower relationships. (Northhouse, 2019)

Are leaders born or made question has been there for a long time and there have been various contributions from theorists and leadership scholars. (Marques,2010; Swaroop,2013). While Henrikson (2006) believes that great leaders are made, Sposato (2024) says it is probably wrong to enquire if leaders are born or made.

The debate seems to continue, however, the answer to whether leaders are born or made, would be a combination of both if leadership is understood to be a resource rather than a process or a skill.

———

The question itself seems to assume that the practice of leadership follows some set patterns that segregates some people with special abilities to lead from the others.

How do leaders emerge? Who can be a leader? Are leaders born or made? There are theories that suggest that some people were born with special abilities that made them into leaders (Yukl,2006) and though there can be some exceptionally talented individuals in leading positions, everyone is born with the ability to learn, think, analyze and act. (Smilkstein, 2004;2011).

Anyone that activates and applies himself to learning (awareness), concern (thoughtfulness) and acts upon such thoughtfulness, can become a real leader, regardless of background.

Since leadership is an innate human resource, it follows naturally that leaders are born with latent leadership. And because leadership activation can be in levels, it could be said that good leaders can be made.

In summary therefore, although everyone is born with latent leadership abilities not all activate their leaderships.

However, leaders can be made when those with latent leadership are influenced or encouraged or trained to activate their latent leadership (leadership-within), and thereby attain leaderhood.

There is a place for training people to become excellent leaders although they were born as leaders in principle, with latent leadership. Therefore, latent leaders are born, and active leaders are self-made by active awareness, concern, and action.

The idea of leaders being specially born has led to eras of people who were hailed as charismatic leaders because they were considered to be special people. (Riggio, 1998; Vergauwe et al., 2018)

In the quest to understand, explain and define leadership, several conflicting results have emerged over a long period of time.

These conflicting ideas have led to much research about the true nature of leadership, yet many questions remain unanswered.

Of these many ideas, about leaders, there are two prominent schools which Dweck (2006) in Chase (2010) identified as the fixed mindset and the growth mindset where the fixed mindset is that which believes in leadership as innate quality, as supposed by the Great Man Theory, and the Traits Theory, while the growth mindset is that which believes that leadership is learnable quality that can be enhanced through habits, skill and training.

In seeking to identify how leaders' performances are shaped Dweck (2006) introduced the leadership mindset which shows that leaders perform according to which of the two schools they belonged. Those who have a fixed mindset would behave differently to those who have a growth mindset, and those with a growth mindset are more likely to learn and develop their leadership skills.

The leadership mindset as laid out by Dweck (2006) explains leadership performance, but the question remains: what is leadership? Is leadership a set of people management skills, a set of traits or some other things? Some scholars claim that leadership is a set of traits or special abilities (Yukl,2006:13) while some others have submitted that Leadership is the process of influencing people to do things to achieve set goals. (Burns,1978; Yukl,2006; Northhouse,2010)

Leadership is widely *believed to be* the process of influencing others to achieve certain goals (Northouse, 2019; Ibrahim and Daniel, 2019) and that suggests that the principal issue in leadership is influence (Barrow, 1977; Gardner, 1995; Kotter, 1998; Vealey, 2005; Northouse, 2010;2019) *but is* influence the principal issue in leadership?

The ability to influence others is a valuable tool in a leader's armoury and it is a necessary skill where goal performance is required but leadership is more than goal achievement tactics or skills.

Looking at leadership as a process of influencing performance seems to reduce leadership to transactional operations and describes better leading tactics and suitable behaviour towards achieving performance. Is leadership only about influencing goal performances?

Even if leadership rallies around the achievement of set goals, what exactly is leadership? Does leadership refer to the efforts we make to get things done? The efforts we make to get things done is better described as 'leadership action' and does not readily tell what leadership itself is.

Leading as a verb tends to describe the efforts we make, while leadership as a noun could mean more than leading. Influencing people to act or achieve performance is an act of leading. Influencing, leading, coordinating can be synonyms referring to the act of a leader in different situations. In broad terms, what has been described by several theories, is leading, rather than leadership.

The Traits theory of leadership suggests that leadership is innate but falls short where it claims that these innate abilities to lead are inherent in some special people, just as 'the Great Man theory' also posits. (Colbert et al., 2012; Maloş 2012; Penney et al., 2015; Mouton 2019).

Several pieces of research have shown that there are no dominant characteristics in many great leaders and so the Traits theory has failed to explain how leadership occurs (Chelladurai,1990) and the learnability of leadership skills tend to support the idea of leadership being the process of influencing performance.

Still, leadership in general terms has not been addressed because learnable leadership skills is different from leadership.

Looking at leadership as the same as learnable leading skills reduces leadership to a set of activities. Leading is an activity. Influencing is an activity. Leadership is not an activity.

Leadership is an innate resource available to everyone, not to just a few special people as claimed in the Great Man theory and the Traits theory.

Understanding what leadership is, in practical terms is important and attempts to define leadership have resulted in conflicting ideas and several questions have arisen as to whether leadership is a set of people management skills, a set of traits or some other things?

Leadership literature is equally replete with conflicting submissions on whether leaders are born or made and there are two visible divides. One school of thought support the view that leaders are born and believe that not everyone can be a leader because some special people with some special talents, gifts or peculiarities emerge as leaders.

In the past, because some individuals performed greatly while leading other people, the assumption arose that those leaders were special people who were born with special and peculiar abilities to lead.

Such leaders were considered as great men with leadership traits while others were considered to have no leadership traits and therefore, only people considered to have been born great became leaders. (Yukl, 2006:13; Colbert et al., 2012; Maloş, 2012; Penney et al., 2015; Mouton, 2019). These beliefs or assumptions are likely based on selective facts of history by looking at many great leaders of the past who undoubtedly demonstrated exceptional abilities.

For a long time, leadership was seen from the lens of that great man endowed with peculiar skills or traits. Research however has shown that many other people have become great and effective leaders despite not having special birth circumstances. (Chelladurai, 1990).

Research has also shown that anyone can be trained to take the lead of any group. An example is that of soldiers who were not born great but rose from the ranks to lead great armies.

Some others see leadership as a process of influencing performance (Burns,1978; Yukl,2006; Northhouse,2010) and point out that others that did not have special talents or peculiarities of birth, have also done well as leaders and they claim that leaders are made through endeavours, trials, necessity, situations, training, exposure, and many other factors. These mostly fall into the classification of advocates of skills and process, and the most notable are those who see leadership as influence.

Mainly, to explain what leadership is, the choice has been between the Traits theory and the 'Process theory of leadership'. Research has not shown sustained or dominant peculiarities in all the leaders of the past, and as such the Traits theory has become a weak argument (Chelladurai,1990) and the "Process theory of leadership" seems to have conveniently filled the gap.

There are other contributions from other theorists and these explanations include emphasis on skills, transformations, authenticity, servanthood, and much more, all in the bid to show how people can be led better, without having leadership traits contrary to the Traits theory.

Despite the weakened position of the Traits theory, and the popularity of the 'Process theory of leadership', leadership remains unexplained in good detail. For example, when it is claimed that "Leadership is the process of influencing people to act towards achieving set goals," it leaves many questions unanswered, and some of such questions are:

- Is leadership the process of influencing performance?
- Who set the goals to be achieved and how did that person arrive at such desired goals?
- Did an individual set the goals to be achieved by others, and if so, is it the setting of the goals that is leadership or the ability to both set goals and get others to achieve such goals
- If the setting of goals is what makes him a leader, is leadership then not

synonymous with the ability to set goals?

- If the setting of goals and ensuring performance, makes a leader, is leadership different from management?

In some quarters, leadership has been projected as the ability to set goals and attain great performances, and many scholars believe that leadership can therefore be taught as skills (Parks 2005; Mole 2010; Ciampa et al., 2010)

The fact that skills of leading can be taught to people should not only be a one-sided proof against the Traits theory, but it can also be supposed that the ability to respond to skills training shows that leading is an innate ability that can be enhance by training and this is what the Leaderhood Theory projects. In this case, leadership is not the innate ability of just a select few, but of everyone.

The fact that people are taught skills for leading and they respond, is a testimony to the ability of everyone to lead, given the right circumstances. And that is where the leaderhood theory through the Leadership Activation Perspective brings a balance by showing that everyone can become leaders because they are born with innate leading traits that are latent at first and then transforms when people activate their innate leadership traits and attain the leaderhood status.

While Dwerk (2006) identified the fixed and growth mindsets, the Leaderhood Theory promotes *a balanced mindset* which is a combination of both the fixed and the growth mindsets. A person with the Balanced Mindset would understand that he and others were born as Latent Leaders and their leading abilities can be enhanced by both activation and skills acquisition.

What should be the conclusion to the question of whether leaders are born or made? The first truth is that everyone is a leader! And as a result, all leaders are born, and every human being has been born with the innate ability to lead.

Leaderhood, through the Leadership Activation Perspective posits that everyone is born to lead, and that this innate ability to lead can be enhanced.

Leadership *as* an innate ability possessed by everyone settles the agelong question of whether leaders are born or made because the leadership activation perspective shows that leaders are born and can be made to be better leaders.

Leadership is inborn and can be activated. However, not everyone has been able to activate or develop the use of their God-given ability to lead. Anyone can become trained in ways of activating their inner leadership and so, they can be made to be good leaders as well as having been born as leaders.

THE LEADER'S SOCIAL BACKGOUND
Literature suggests that personality and social background sometimes dictate who becomes a leader and who does not become a leader (Zaccaro et al., 2008; Martins et al., 2017; Asselman et al., (2023)

Is nobility truly the test of leadership emergence? Are there some traits that preclude some people but entrench some in leading positions? All these have been researched by scholars and the results are divers. (Ridgeway, 2001; McClean et al., 2018; Lianidou and Zheng, 2023). There are claims that personality does not determine leadership emergence or behaviour (Spangler &House, 2004)

What should be the real place of nobility and other social conditions of birth like family, social standing, or education on the emergence as leader? Research has indicated some relationships between social standing and emergence as leaders. (Duan et al.,2022).

The error of attributing leading positions to traits, personality, and other conditions of birth, arise because of misunderstanding of what leadership is.

Leadership itself is an innate resource possessed by all, rather than a process.

What has been described in literature and labelled as leadership is at best, 'leadership practice' or in simple terms, 'leading'. Leadership (innate resource) makes leading (external activity) possible.

While conditions of birth, personality, traits, and other factors could affect the level and pace of leadership activation, these do not specify leadership. (Spangler and House,2004).

Possibly, those of commendable backgrounds could be accustomed to taking leader-like decisions but it does not infer that everyone from commendable backgrounds are automatic leaders in comparison to others from other backgrounds.

Background, personality, traits, social status can affect:

- How a person thinks
- How aware a person would be
- How concerned a person would be
- How a person act

Leaderhood however, supersedes background. Take the example of two people from different backgrounds.

The one from a noble background could activate leadership earlier due to being used to free expression and other liberties while the one from a less noble background could be slower in activating leadership, possibly due to some complex, including:

- Inferiority
- Fear of non-acceptance
- Fear of making mistakes

However, the moment each of these two people activate their leaderships, they can operate as leaders in their own rights. Although literature seems to suggest that backgrounds affect followers' perception of leaders (Goldfien et al., 2024) but it remains researchable how much background, affects the level of leadership activation.

People do not live in the isolation of others. There are relationships between people in society and some people lead and some people follow. Leading in social circles is not so different to leading in business or politics.

Most leadership situations have to do with
the use of power and control and that has
elements of politics in it.

8

THE MECHANISMS OF LEADING POLITICS

LEADING SPECTRUM

Leading can occur at individual, team, organisation, and societal levels, and this could be with or without official power.

The emergence of the leader is usually by appointment or through some social engineering. (Guastello,2007) and that follows some processes, however in some cases, some people become leaders by accident or impose themselves on others. (Bracey, 2007; Momin, 2018)

Everyone could become leaders upon activating their leadership. Current followers are potential leaders because they have latent leadership within them. Current leaders can be real leaders.

Current followers and current leaders have Leadership within them, but all cannot be leaders at the same time. As discussed earlier, attaining leaderhood positions a person as potential leader.

All of us are not leaders at the same level all the time. At any given time, some would be leaders, and some would be followers.

Regarding Leaders and Followers, there is a scope of interrelatedness, and this forms neatly into a leadership spectrum of four classes:

(1) Leaders among Leaders

(2) Followers among Leaders

(3) Leaders among Followers

(4) Followers among Followers

These four classes of leaders activate their leadership differently.

The fact that a person is seen as a Follower does not mean he is not a "Leader", in his own space.

Many people are not seen as leaders, but they possess and display leadership as chance presents itself especially if they already attained leaderhood. Do we then say they became leaders overnight? No, but they are leaders-in-waiting by virtue of their leadership activation.

Even among Leaders, they also look up to some others for Leadership. And in such cases, Leaders become Followers.
A husband is a leader in his house, yet he could be a follower at work!

The politics of leading involves all forms of leadership situations related to the use of influence and power. What happens mostly at work is 'leadership' politics, but leadership is described as the process of influencing people to act towards achieving goal performance, (Ibrahim and Daniel,2019; Northouse,2019) and this description seems to fit better in describing leading politics at work.

Leading politics is everywhere but could vary slightly in non-work situations at social, religious, or political levels.

Whether for work or non-work situations, leading politics involve the activation of one's leadership for political goals(headship) and involves a great mix of

- Political Awareness
- Political Concern
- Political Action

The essence of leading politics is power, and it is usually about:

- Attaining Power
- Sustaining Power
- Perpetuating Power

Depending on the circumstances, several tools can be used in achieving power and includes:

- Influence
- Money
- Race
- Religion
- Force

Apart from gaining the control of power, those in leading positions find themselves making diverse decisions for and on behalf members of their groups. They make policies and they decide the future directions of the group. It is important to note that the leader's behaviour has impacts on policy, social change, and development. Policy inputs lead to policy outcomes and policy inputs could depend on the quality, style, and actions of those in-charge.

Leading politics also involves the balancing of the leader-follower relationships in ways that the followers buy-in into the ideas, policies, and leadings of the leaders. Getting followers to toe a particular line could involve:

- **Negotiations** – as usual with democratic leaders
- **Manipulations** – as usual with charismatic leaders
- **Coercion** – as usual with autocratic or dictatorial leaders
- **Guidance** - as usual with real leaders.

As previously mentioned, what is described and discussed as leadership in various literature are issues relating to the politics of leading. Leadership presented in literature, as the process of influencing people to pursue and achieve set goals, is basically describing leading politics.

Leadership in general does not start and end with influence or power over others but starts with having an inward reflection on situations and issues.

Internal leadership activation precedes external leading. A person needs to lead himself first to activate his leadership before looking to influence others.

LEADERS' LEADING STYLES
Much has been written about different managing styles of people in charge of organisations and these have been tagged as leadership styles. However, the Leadership Activation Perspective distinguishes leading from leadership, and finds it appropriate to discuss leading styles rather than leadership styles, since leadership is a resource.

When leading people and organisations is based on the use of power, different leaders deploy varied means and styles to lead, and these could generally fall into one of the following:

- **Populist style**

This involves pandering to the followers. A leader in this situation has deep awareness of the issues faced by his followers, and he can show his concern vividly as well as the ability to make things happen. Everything such a leader does is to win the applause of the followers. This kind of leader will likely have a high level of leadership activation through which he has mastered the needs of his followers and tailors his leading efforts towards satisfying them.

In practical terms this style could have the elements of democratic principles and people have the rights to partake in the decision-making process.

Most Politicians use the populist style, especially when they are new in office and desire the affection of the electorate. Even in business settings, new leaders tend to be populist.

- **Commando style**

This is a style used by some dictatorial heads and rulers. They care less about being popular with the followers so far as they can achieve their desired goals. Those who use this style rely heavily on their official power which they invoke from time to time. Such people make no pretensions about their instructions which must be followed. It is either their way or the highway.

In this style, the leaders are larger than life and act as mini gods, who cannot be challenged. Such people do not care what anyone thinks about them or their leadership ability. Their main focus is performance, and they achieve that through rules, regulations, decrees and sometimes the use of force.

- **Bandit style**

In this kind of political leadership style, those in leading positions tend to take their followers hostages.

They hold the four aces! They have control of all form of infrastructures and processes. They do as they like without having regard to repercussions because usually, there are none.

Such leaders make difficult rules and set up procedures that the followers cannot escape from following. They are not real dictators but show dictatorial tendencies. Such leaders would tend to micromanage their followers, giving them no breathing spaces for personal initiatives.

In this kind of style, the leader is unpredictable and springs surprises at will. Since there are no defined operational parameters for leading in this kind of style, whatever the leader does is the right thing.

In any organisation, including faith-based organisations, political parties, social groups, the understanding of the political aspects of leading is crucial.

The basis of power and the attendant influence emanating from that power differs depending on the source of such power.

The power and influence over people of faith would come from their religious dogmas, books, and doctrines. And even the most incompetent person appointed to lead would wield enormous power because of the inherent influence in his position.

In similar ways, the power and influence over political party members, club members, citizens would come from their constitutions. The power and influence of the boss over other workers would come from the office or position held.

Holding office or being in powerful positions make people become the heads of such organisations but they could be deficient in 'leadership' unless and until they attain leaderhood, through leadership activation.

Some organisations end up in chaos when they appoint leaders who do not have leadership activation.

And they try to fix the situation by sending such heads on 'leadership training'. Such trainings focus on how to manage people but is mistaken for leadership development.

People cannot be trained to be leaders. People are leaders from birth but can be trained to activate their leadership or to become better at leading. People can be trained to become deliberately interested in issues, to become aware, to become concerned and show more concern, and to follow their awareness and concerns with right actions.

People should be trained to understand their inner leadership abilities and how to communicate these.

Leaders are involved with making policies and it should be noted that policy input leads directly or indirectly to policy outcomes, which could be either positive or negative. Policy input depends on the quality, style, and behaviour of leaders.

9

LEADERSHIP FAILURE

WHAT IS LEADERSHIP FAILURE?
When things do not go the way they should,
in groups or societies, people adduce
'leadership failure' as the reason for such
deplorable performances and by that they
mean that the failures have been due to the
lack of proper management on the part of the
leaders.

Often, people blame inefficiencies and
inadequate performances on leadership
failure and by that they mean that those in
leadership positions have failed to lead well.

It is not untrue that those leading could fail
but why they have failed should be linked to
the nature of their leadership activations
individually and corporately. Leadership
failure is not about the performance of
leaders but about the absence of leadership
in its correct proportions.

What constitutes leadership failure? Leaderhood theory takes the view that leadership is an innate resource available to everyone, and that leadership failure goes beyond issues of performance and effectiveness. Although the results of leadership failure would include bad performance and ineffectiveness, leadership failure is not about poor performances.

According to Leaderhood Theory, Leadership failure will result under three conditions:

- Absence of leadership activation
- Absence of leadership fit
- Absence of leadership equilibrium

Let us look at these three reasons for leadership failure:

ABSENCE OF LEADERSHIP ACTIVATION

According to Leaderhood theory, until the latent leadership in a person is activated, such a person cannot exercise leadership. Where leaders are appointed but they have no awareness of issues, no concern for the status quo and how to change the situation, and they have not taken actions to change the situation, there is a failure of leadership. The leadership within them, (that innate resource) has failed to achieve results.

What happens in the absence of leadership activation?
In a group setting that consists of those who have not activated their leadership, such a group would be a rudderless bunch of people because they have not attained leaderhood and therefore, the latent leadership in them has failed to activate.

Such groups could eventually experience chaotic ideas, chaotic projects, chaotic relationships, and chaotic structures full of confusing motions and lack of progress. Such groups could be family units, institutions, government organizations or even nations.

The absence of leadership activation represents the absence of initiatives, absence of vision and outright absence of direction, even when someone is placed there as a leader.

Such groups find themselves revolving around issues without being able to find real solutions. Such groups tend to expend time, energy, and resources in the wrong directions, yet they would expect progress.

For any group, therefore, to make appreciable progress, there should be in that group, a crop of those that have attained leaderhood which is demonstrable by awareness of issues at stake; a concern for status quo and the necessity to progress; as well as the capabilities to take actions towards achieving progress.

In some instances, some groups are populated by a vast majority of those who have not activated their leadership and the few that have activated their leadership are seen as 'demigods' and are said to be charismatic leaders. Charisma is nothing more than leadership opportunism.

Even among leaders, the levels of enthusiasm differ. Some are reluctant leaders who got leading positions by accident (Duan et al., 2022).

The basis of their appointment could be political or administrative and such leaders could be complacent. On the other side are the enthusiastic leaders who got leading positions by intention, quest, or ambition. The basis of such leaders' appointments or emergence could be interest in issues or professional competence.

Individuals differ and so are the levels of enthusiasm about anything in life, including leading positions. Even enthusiastic leaders could be different in their levels of enthusiasm and that enthusiastic use of leadership (resource), is often mistaken as charisma.

Levels of enthusiasm could be mild, high, or even excessive, depending on individual personality. Literature on Charisma is vast, and it is thought that some leaders have charisma while others do not. (Riggio, 1998; Vergauwe et al., 2018).

The Leadership Activation Perspective sees Charisma as advanced leadership activation in disguise.

When a person is aware and thinks about issues and becomes concerned about such issues, and makes some effort to resolve the issues, then others tag them as having charisma. In that sense, charisma is activated leadership at levels beyond the average. And because less people activate their latent leaderships, those who have activated their leadership are labeled as having charisma.

Charisma requires the desire to see better results. Charisma also involves the putting of efforts to see such desired results. Possibly because many people do not care or do not have an awareness of better possibilities, they do nothing but rely on the few whom they label as being charismatic.

Charisma is personal and can hardly be duplicated. Each person has different levels of charisma and the judge of these levels of charisma are those affected by their influences either directly or indirectly.

Charisma would be the effect of perception from the point of view of those who idolize people in position, authority, or power.

Perception plays a crucial role in deciding how charismatic a person is and there are two blocs to this. One bloc could see a 'charismatic' person as one who is ordained to lead or equipped to lead, but the other bloc could see a charismatic person as 'the messiah', (the only one that could lead).

Charisma could depend on how popular a person has become. People become popular for varied reasons aside from leading. People could confuse charisma with popularity or fame. For example, a film star could easily influence his fans, not because of any charisma but because of his aura, personality, or the love they have for him.

When aura or love for a leader is confused with charisma, people likely become blind followers and sycophants and could find out much later about that leader that there has been no activated leadership but just influence.

This leads to 'leadership cults', where followers can go to any length to defend the errors of those leading them and this is common in politics.

Yet those leading them have only fame that has been confused with charisma. If countries rely on power and charisma to choose their leaders, such people could win elections but might not perform well.

Leading at any level, without attaining leaderhood (leadership activation) is a mark of leadership failure, regardless of how charismatic the leader appears to be.

ABSENCE OF LEADERSHIP FIT

Imagine asking a toddler to drive a car. That would be asking the impossible. Or imagine asking a car driver to drive an armoured truck when his license is just for a car. That would be asking for too much because the skill is not a fit for the role. This is the same with Leadership fit.

Leadership fit is measured in individual terms and is characterized by proportionate leadership activation in relation to leadership need. Where the leadership needs do not tally with the deployed leadership activation, there is no leadership fit and that signifies leadership failure.

Lack of leadership fit can be due to either inadequate or surplus activation.
Leadership fit can be described as having a round peg in a round hole as far as deployment of leadership is concerned. When there has been an unbalanced deployment of leadership efforts to issues and situations, then there is no leadership fit.

When an individual's leadership activation is casual or basic, there is a limit to how much leadership can be provided by them. A person with limited casual or basic leadership activation is a leader but would be effective where projects or situations are basic and at the level of his leadership activation.

It would be a misfit where a person with casual leadership activation is assigned to lead a complex situation. In such a case, the available leadership activation will be below the level of leadership required and so, there is no leadership fit. Such a leader becomes overwhelmed and that lack of leadership-fit leads to underperformance.

On the other hand, when a person with intense or deep leadership activation is assigned to lead in a simple and basic situation, there is no leadership fit. Although that leader could still perform well above what is required, but he will perform below his level of leadership ability. Such leaders could become mistaken for or seen as a superhero or a charismatic performer while he only performed below his leadership activation level. It is like a Postgraduate student asked to recite A, B, C... (English alphabets).

The more intense or advanced the level of leadership activation, the better the quality of leadership offered. The leadership needed for simple situations would not be as stringent as that needed for complex situations. The absence of leadership-fit signifies leadership failure.

ABSENCE OF LEADERSHIP EQUILIBRIUM
The overall pool of leaders in an organisation is referred to as "the leadership".

Organisations usually measure their performances based on several factors, but they hardly appraise their overall leadership stock. How sustainable an organisation is in the long run could depend on the quantity, quality and the balance of leadership it has. Leadership is personal. Leadership activation is also personal; however, the level of leadership activation of a person could have great implications for their organisation. Corporate Leadership, (as aggregate activated leaderhood) could be in equilibrium or in disequilibrium.

Leadership disequilibrium is an indication of a failure of leadership, as a resource, because despite the group being populated by those who have attained leaderhood, the leadership resources of the group in aggregate terms, have failed to support the group's leadership needs appropriately.

Leadership is in equilibrium at the point where the level of leadership required equates with the right level of leadership. At least four possibilities exist:

1. **PERFECT HIGH EQUILIBRIUM** Where high level of leadership requirement is met with a high level of leadership ability, there is perfect high equilibrium. At this stage the level of leadership is advanced and mature for what it is set to achieve.

2. **PERFECT LOW EQUILIBRIUM** Where low level of leadership requirement is met with low level of leadership ability, there is perfect low equilibrium. At this stage, the leadership activation is basic and rudimentary but sufficient for what it is set to achieve.

3. **NEGATIVE DISEQUILIBRIUM** Where high level of leadership requirement is met with a low level of leadership ability, in corporate terms. At this level there is a leadership gap in the organisation and mediocrity is not far

away. In such an instance, "leadership expansion" is recommended. The leaders involved would need to increase and expand their leadership activation by expanding their thought-bands; getting more involved by asking questions; researching; familiarising with issues; understanding the gaps and working towards bridging identified gaps. These gaps could be in terms of communication gaps, relationship gaps and activity gaps.

4. **POSITIVE DISEQUILIBRIUM** Where low level of leadership requirement is met with a high level of leadership, there is disequilibrium, but this disequilibrium is positive because the available aggregate leadership is above par with requirement. This could be due to having one or more leaders who have excess activations beyond the needs of the organisation or due to the combined excess activations of all the leaders.

At the positive disequilibrium stage, the leaders concerned are likely to be overqualified or over experienced for the roles they lead, or the organisation has a top-heavy load of leaders. This has implications at both individual and corporate levels.

Positive disequilibrium at individual level is the same as having absence of leadership-fit and could be good for the individual performances of such leaders but if this persist, it could lead to situations where those leaders become 'tin gods' and either becomes 'worshipped' by others in the organisation or they demand to be better recognised and when that fails, such leaders could exit the organisation and that is a minus to the organisation. This possibly explains partially, why some people in organisations look up to some 'charismatic leaders'. They are possibly "charismatic" because they have a higher level of leadership activation than needed.

For sustainability, where there is positive disequilibrium, measured at individual levels, such a leader's role should be matched with equal assignments, possibly through job enlargement or giving more responsibilities or equally higher roles.

Where there is leadership disequilibrium in an organisation, that signifies leadership failure. Leadership failure therefore could exist at both individual and corporate levels.

CLOSING REMARKS

In the following pages you will see some suggestions on:

"HOW TO BE A GREATER LEADER"

You have studied leadership up until this stage and that is a great achievement by itself.

No doubts, you are a leader already whether you hold a leading position or not. Even if you are a leader at this time, it is possible that you are a great leader, and you can become a greater leader.

Many people desiring to be great leaders have attended many courses tagged "leadership courses" or "leadership development courses" and while these are great investments of time and resources, there are no ways of measuring that they have become greater leaders than they were before attending such courses.

Possibly they could become better managers but not necessarily great leaders.

Can a leader be trained to become a great leader? Maybe we should first define who a great leader is. A great leader would be that leader that is able to do three things:

1. Motivate himself to activate his leadership continually
2. Apply his leadership activation to situations and thereby achieve desired results
3. Motivate others to activate their leaderships

Before anyone can be a great leader, he or she must first be a leader in the real sense of it, that is: attain leaderhood by engaging the four drivers of leadership. Thereafter such a leader should be able to use more initiatives to continue repeating the leadership cycle of activation, action, performance, and review until leadership maturity is attained, and thereby impact his performance, the organisational performance, and the leadership activation of others.

BECOMING A GREATER LEADER

There are no general rules, but the following suggestions should be helpful if you want to become a greater leader:

If you want to be a great leader do the following five things:

- **Audit yourself**
- **Improve**
- **Seek help**
- **Develop others**
- **Be nice**

AUDIT YOURELF

You are your own champion. You are your best critic because you will tell yourself the truth. No other person can truly understand you or your mind or your moves. Therefore, you are the best person to mark your own script.

You will do well to ask yourself some of the following and the answers will show you the gaps you need to cover. When you cover those gaps, your leadership activation should improve significantly and then, being a great leader is just a matter of time.

1. **Understand what leadership is and be sure you have attained leaderhood status.**
   o Am I exercising my **Thoughts** appropriately on issues at hand?
   o Do I have enough **Awareness** about issues on hand and their conditions?
   o Am I **Concern**ed about the issues on hand? Do I sincerely care about the issues on hand? How much do I care? How much can I care?
   o Have I taken any **Action**? What steps can I take change the situation? What can I do to make things better? What steps have I taken so far?

2. **Identify what kind of leader you are:**
   o Am I a Leader of Thoughts?
   o Am I a leader of Processes?
   o Am I a leader of Practice?
   o Am I unsure of what I am?

3. **Thoughts, Processes, and Practice are important areas where a leader's activation can be concentrated**
    - o In which of these three areas am I better?
    - o In which of these three areas am I poor?
    - o How can I improve my activation in Thoughts?
    - o How can I improve my activation in Processes?
    - o How can I improve my activation in Practice?

4. **What are my limitations and how can I overcome them?**
    - o What can limit my thoughts? Am I stable enough to think about these issues?
    - o What is limiting my awareness? Am I outgoing? Do I seek relevant information?
    - o What is limiting my concern? Nonchalance? Indifference?
    - o What is limiting my action? Fear? Complex? Indifference?

IMPROVE

No matter how great you currently are, you can be greater and that could require improvements in some areas. The following should be improved if you want to be a greater leader:

1. **Increase your use of initiatives-** Be self-motivated.

2. **Increase your leadership activation –** Apply yourself to more thoughts, do more research (read more, ask more questions, seek more information), be more concerned and take more action

3. **Improve your communications –** Share your ideas rather than giving commands.

SEEK HELP

Surely you know a lot and you can do so much but you cannot know all the answers to all issues, always. Seek the cooperation of others by asking them to cooperate with what you have already shared with them. By asking for help, you are indirectly training your followers to do the same. Cooperation is better than competition.

DEVELOP OTHERS

A good leader seeks to replace himself with more leaders. One of your targets is to support your followers to also activate their leaderships. As a leader, you should worry less about performances but concentrate more on upgrading and developing your followers. These followers will perform because their leadership have been awakened.

BE NICE!

No matter your position or title, be nice to others especially your followers. Nobody loves a nasty person. People might not react when their leaders are nasty or bossy, because of fear. However, when they have the opportunity, they would sabotage such a leader. Remember that everyone has leadership potential and any of the followers can become a great leader.

You can become a Certified Leader.

Visit **www.certified-leaders.com** for further details.

References

Asselmann, E., Holst, E. and Specht, J. (2023) Longitudinal bidirectional associations between personality and becoming a leader. *Journal of personality*, 91(2), pp.285-298.

Barrow, J.C. (1977) The variables of leadership: A review and conceptual framework. *Academy of Management Review,* 2,233-251.

Bolden, R. (2004) *What is leadership?.* Centre for Leadership Studies, University of Exeter.

Bracey, M. (2007) The accidental leader. *Leading work with young people*, pp.25-33.

Burns, J.M. (1978) Leadership. New York: Harper & Row.

Bush, T. (2020) Theories of educational leadership and management.

Chase, M. (2010) Should Coaches Believe In Innate Ability? The Importance of Leadership Mindset. Quest. 62.296-307.

Chelladurai, P. (1990) Leadership in sports: A review. International Journal of Sports Psychology, 21(4), 328-354.

Cheng, Y.C. (2002) Leadership and strategy. *The principles and practice of educational management*, pp.51-69.

Ciampa, E.J., Hunt, A.A. and Dermody, T.S. (2010) Leadership can and should be taught. *Academic Medicine, 85*(12), p.1814.

Colbert, A.E., Judge, T.A., Choi, D. and Wang, G. (2012) Assessing the trait theory of leadership using self and observer ratings of personality: The mediating role of contributions to group success. *The leadership quarterly, 23*(4), pp.670-685.

Cole, G.A. and Kelly, P. (2015) *Management theory and practice* (p. 624). Boston, Massachusetts: Cengage Learning.

Covey, S.M. and Merrill, R.R. (2006) *The speed of trust: The one thing that changes everything.* Simon and schuster.

Daft, R.L. (2005) The leadership experience (3rd ed.). Mason, OH: Thomson, South-Western.

Duan, J., Ren, X., Liu, Z. and Riggio, R.E. (2022) Connecting the dots: How parental and current socioeconomic status shape individuals' transformational leadership. *Journal of Business Research, 150*, pp.51-58.

Dweck, C.S. (2006) *Mindset: The new psychology of success(pp.108-143).* New York: Random House

Gardner, H. (1995) *Leading minds: An anatomy of leadership*. New York: Basic Books.

Goldfien, M., Joseph, M. and Krcmaric, D. (2024) When do leader backgrounds matter? Evidence from the President's Daily Brief. *Conflict Management and Peace Science*, *41*(4), pp.414-437.

Guastello, S.J. (2007) How leaders really emerge. *American Psychologist*, Vol 62(6), pp.606-607

Henrikson, M. (2006) Great leaders are made, not born. *Nursing for Women's Health*, *10*(4), pp.335-338.

Houpt, J.L., Gilkey, R.W., Ehringhaus, S.H., Houpt, J.L., Gilkey, R.W. and Ehringhaus, S.H. (2015) Personality Traits and Leadership. *Learning to Lead in the Academic Medical Center: A Practical Guide*, pp.35-44.

Ibrahim, A. U. and Daniel, C.O. (2019) Impact of leadership on organisational performance. International Journal of Business, Management and Social Research, 06(02), pp. 367-374.

Kellerman, B. (2008) How followers are creating change and changing leaders. *Harvard Business School*.

Kotter, J.P. (1990) *A Force for Change: How Leadership Differs from Management.* New York: Free Press

Kotter, J.P. (1998) What leaders really do. In *Harvard Business Review* on leadership (pp.37-60). Boston: Harvard Business School Press

Kotter, J.P. (2008) *Force for change: How leadership differs from management.* Simon and Schuster.

Kotterman, J. (2006) Leadership versus management: what's the difference?. *The Journal for Quality and Participation,* 29(2), p.13.

Kouzes, J.M. and Posner, B.Z. (2023) *The leadership challenge: How to make extraordinary things happen in organizations.* John Wiley & Sons.

Lianidou, T. and Zheng, W. (2023) Leader diffuse status and leadership outcomes: towards an integrative framework. *International Journal of Management Reviews,* 25(3), pp.443-466.

Maloş, R. (2012) THE MOST IMPORTANT LEADERSHIP THEORIES. *Annals of Eftimie Murgu University Resita, Fascicle II, Economic Studies.*

Marques, J.F. (2010) Awakened leaders: born or made? *Leadership & Organization Development Journal*, 31(4), pp.307-323.

Matthews, S.H., Kelemen, T.K. and Bolino, M.C. (2021) How follower traits and cultural values influence the effects of leadership. *The Leadership Quarterly*, 32(1), p.101497.

McClean, E.J., Martin, S.R., Emich, K.J. and Woodruff, C.T. (2018) The social consequences of voice: An examination of voice type and gender on status and subsequent leader emergence. *Academy of Management Journal*, 61(5), pp.1869-1891.

Mintzberg, H. (1998) Retrospective commentary on the manager's job: Folklore and fact. In *Harvard Business Review* on leadership (pp.29-32). Boston: Harvard Business School Press

Mole, G. (2010) Can leadership be taught? In *Leadership in organizations* (pp. 126-138). Routledge.

Momin, Z. (2018) Accidental captains. *Asian Management Insights*, 5(2), pp.12-17.

Mouton, N. (2019) A literary perspective on the limits of leadership: Tolstoy's critique of the great man theory. *Leadership*, 15(1), pp.81-102.

Northouse, P.G. (2010) Leadership: Theory and practice (5th ed.). Thousand Oaks, CA: Sage.

Northouse, P.G. (2019) *Leadership: Theory&Practice,* Los Angeles: Sage Publications

Parks, S.D. (2005) *Leadership can be taught: A bold approach for a complex world.* Harvard Business Review Press.

Penney, S.A., Kelloway, E.K. and O'Keefe, D. (2015) Trait theories of leadership. In *Leadership in sport* (pp. 19-33). Routledge

Piccolo, R.F. and Buengeler, C. (2013) Leadership and goal setting. In *New developments in goal setting and task performance* (pp. 357-374). Routledge.

Ridgeway, C.L. (2001) Gender, status, and leadership. *Journal of Social issues, 57*(4), pp.637-655.

Riggio, R.E. (1998) Charisma. *Encyclopedia of mental health, 1,* pp.387-396.

Rost, J. (1993) *Leadership for the twenty-first century.* Bloomsbury Publishing USA.

Rowe, W.G. (2001) Creating wealth in organizations: The role of strategic leadership. *Academy of Management Executive,* 15(1), 81-94.

Smilkstein, R. (2004) August. Born to be creative and critical thinkers. In *Imaginative Education Research Group Conference, Vancouver, BC Retrieved Dec* (Vol. 23, p. 2007).

Smilkstein, R. (2011) *We're born to learn: Using the brain's natural learning process to create today's curriculum.* Corwin Press.

Spangler, W.D. and House, R.J. (2004) Personality and leadership. In *Personality and organizations* (pp. 275-314). Psychology Press.

Sposato, M. (2024) Are leaders born or made? Asking the right question. *Development and Learning in Organizations: An International Journal, 38*(3), pp.1-3.

Swaroop, K.R. and Prasad, N.G.A. (2013) Are leaders born or made. *Asia Pacific Journal of Marketing & Management Review ISSN, 2319,* p.2836.

Vealey, R.S. (2005) *Coaching for inneredge* (pp.75-103). Morgantown, WV. Fitness Information Technology.

Vergauwe, J., Wille, B., Hofmans, J., Kaiser, R.B. and De Fruyt, F. (2018) Too much charisma can make leaders look less effective. In *Leadership presence* (pp. 1-6). Harvard Business Review Press.

Xu, A.J., Loi, R., Cai, Z. and Liden, R.C. (2019) Reversing the lens: How followers influence leader–member exchange quality. *Journal of Occupational and Organizational Psychology*, 92(3), pp.475-497.

Yukl, G. (2006) *Leadership in organisations* (6th ed.). Upper Saddle River, NJ: Pearson-Prentice Hall.

Zaccaro, S.J., Gulick, L.M. and Khare, V.P. (2008) Personality and leadership. *Leadership at the crossroads, 1*, pp.13-29

Zalenik, A. (1977) Manager and leaders: Are they different? *Harvard Business Review, 55*, 67-78